This Book Belongs To

Contents

Contents

Contents

Contents

Starters & Canapés

At the beginning of a meal, appetites tend to be at their height, so it is important to choose your starter carefully. This chapter contains a huge variety of recipes to fit in with any dinner menu, and includes hot and cold dishes chosen from cuisines from all around the world. Whatever the occasion, you will find recipes here to whet the appetite of even the most discerning dinner and party guests.

Baked mushrooms

serves 4

ingredients

8 large flat mushrooms, wiped with damp kitchen paper
2 tablespoons olive oil 250g/9oz Taleggio or Brie
cheese, thickly sliced
1 bunch of fresh lemon thyme, leaves only
salt and freshly ground black pepper

- Preheat the oven to 200°C/ 400°F/Gas mark 6.
- Trim the stalks from the mushrooms. Put the mushrooms, rounded cap side down, in a medium roasting dish. Season with salt and pepper.
- Pour the olive oil over the mushrooms. Place the cheese slices on top, and finally sprinkle with the lemon thyme. Bake in the oven for 20-25 minutes until the cheese has melted. Serve hot.

Grilled asparagus & leeks

serves 4

ingredients

12 small leeks, trimmed, with ends removed
12 fresh asparagus spears
olive oil for brushing
50g/2oz pecorino or Parmesan cheese, freshly grated
2 tablespoons freshly squeezed lemon juice

- Preheat the grill to high.
- Arrange the leeks and asparagus in a single layer in a shallow baking dish.
- Brush the vegetables with the olive oil, and place under the grill. Cook for 5-8 minutes, turning occasionally and brushing with more oil as needed.
- When almost done, sprinkle with two-thirds of the grated cheese and all of the lemon juice. Grill for a further minute.
- Finally, sprinkle the remaining cheese on top, and serve hot in the baking dish.

Beetroot & yogurt salad

serves 4

ingredients

350g/12oz cooked beetroot, chopped into bite-sized cubes
2 large gherkins, chopped into large chunks
4 tablespoons Greek-style yogurt 2 tablespoons white wine vinegar
salt and freshly ground black pepper
1 tablespoon finely chopped fresh dill, to garnish

- Put the beetroot and gherkins in a large serving bowl.
- In a separate bowl, mix together the yogurt and vinegar, and season with salt and pepper.
- Pour this mixture over the beetroot and gherkins, and stir. Sprinkle with fresh dill and serve.

Leek kuftadas

serves 4-6

ingredients

700g/1½lb leeks,
trimmed and thinly sliced
175g/6oz feta cheese,
crumbled 3 eggs, beaten
50g/2oz fresh breadcrumbs
4 tablespoons vegetable oil

- Steam the leeks for 4 minutes in a colander or steamer over a pan of boiling water. Remove from the heat and leave to cool.
- In a large bowl, combine the cooled leeks, feta cheese, eggs and breadcrumbs.
- Using a tablespoon of the mixture at a time, mould it into round patties with your hands.
- Heat the oil in a shallow heavy frying pan over a high heat. Shallow-fry the paties for about 5 minutes on each side or until golden brown, cooking in batches if necessary. Drain on kitchen paper, and serve warm.

Tomatoes on toast

serves 4

ingredients

olive oil for brushing and drizzling
6 large tomatoes, thickly sliced
4 thick slices of brown bread
balsamic vinegar for drizzling
50g/2oz Parmesan cheese, shaved
salt and freshly ground black pepper

- Brush a heavy frying pan with oil, and place over a high heat.
- Add the tomato slices and fry them for 3 minutes, turning once until soft and slightly blackened.
- Meanwhile, lightly toast the bread under a grill or in a toaster.
- Put the tomatoes on the warm toast. Drizzle each portion with a little olive oil and balsamic vinegar. Sprinkle with the Parmesan cheese shavings, season with salt and pepper, and serve immediately.

Roast garlic toast

serves 6

ingredients

1 ciabatta loaf
2 whole garlic bulbs
2 tablespoons extra virgin olive oil
5 sprigs of fresh rosemary salt and freshly ground black pepper

- Preheat grill to high.
- Slice off the tops of the garlic bulbs. Leave the cloves whole with their skins on.
- Brush with some of the olive oil. Wrap the garlic bulbs in foil with 3 sprigs of the rosemary. Grill for 25 minutes, turning occasionally.
- Slice the bread and brush each slice with olive oil, then lightly toast both sides under the hot grill.
- Squeeze the garlic cloves from their skins onto the toast.
- Chop the leaves of the remaining rosemary sprigs, and sprinkle over the toast. Season with salt and pepper. Drizzle with the remaining olive oil, and serve warm or hot.

Sweet potato salad

serves 4

ingredients

4 sweet potatoes, peeled and chopped into cubes
3 tablespoons vinaigrette (see page 727)
salt and freshly ground black pepper
2 spring onions, finely chopped
1 small bunch of fresh chives, chopped
pinch of cayenne pepper
2 tablespoons chopped fresh flat-leaf parsley

- Put the sweet potatoes in a heavy saucepan of boiling water. Cook for 10 minutes or until tender, taking care not to overcook. Drain.
- Transfer the warm sweet potatoes to a large bowl, and pour the vinaigrette over the top. Season with salt and pepper, and leave to cool.
- Once the sweet potatoes have cooled, mix in the spring onions and chives. Sprinkle with the pinch of cayenne and the parsley. Serve at room temperature.

Jerusalem artichokes

serves 4

ingredients

908g/2lb round Jerusalem artichokes
3 garlic cloves, crushed
2 tablespoons chopped fresh flat-leaf parsley
2 tablespoons olive oil squeeze of lemon juice salt

• Peel the artichokes, and boil for 8-10 minutes in slightly salted water. Drain in a colander, and place on serving dishes.

• Meanwhile, mix together the garlic, parsley, olive oil and lemon juice. Season with salt. Drizzle the dressing over the warm artichokes, and serve immediately.

Melon & strawberries

serves 4

ingredients

¼ honeydew melon
½ cantaloupe melon 150ml/5fl oz rosé wine
3 teaspoons rose water
175g/6oz small strawberries, rinsed and hulled

• Halve the melons. Scoop out the seeds from both melons using a spoon. Carefully remove the peel.

• Cut the melon flesh into thin strips, and put in a bowl. Pour over the wine and rose water. Mix together, cover and leave to chill in the refrigerator for at least 2 hours.

• Halve the strawberries and mix in with the melon. Allow to stand at room temperature for about 15 minutes before serving.

Onion rings

serves 4-6

ingredients

350ml/12fl oz plain flour
4 tablespoons cornmeal
4 tablespoons onion powder 2 teaspoons salt
350ml/12fl oz milk
1 large egg
8 large onions
vegetable oil for deep-frying

- Combine the flour, cornmeal, onion powder, salt, milk, egg and 125ml/4fl oz water in a large bowl. Stir well until there are no lumps and the batter is smooth.
- Slice the onions across to make rings about 1cm/½in thick.
- Heat the oil in a large saucepan until hot. Test to see whether the oil is hot enough by dropping a little of the batter into the oil - it should sizzle straight away.
- Dip the separated rings into the batter. Drop the coated rings into the oil and fry until golden brown. Cook in batches if necessary.
- Remove the onion rings with a slotted spoon, and drain on kitchen paper. Serve hot.

Mozzarella sticks

serves 4

ingredients

2 eggs, beaten
50ml/2fl oz water 350ml/12fl
oz coarse dried
white breadcrumbs
½ teaspoon garlic salt
1 teaspoon mixed spice
150ml/5fl oz flour
75ml/3fl oz cornflour vegetable
oil for deep-frying 450g/1lb
mozzarella cheese,
cut into finger-size sticks

- Whisk the eggs with 50ml/2fl oz water and set aside. Mix the breadcrumbs, garlic salt and mixed spice together, and set aside. Blend the flour with the cornflour.
- Heat enough vegetable oil for deep-frying in a heavy saucepan. Dredge the cheese sticks in the flour mixture, then dip in the egg. Lastly, coat in the breadcrumb mixture.
- Lower carefully into the hot oil, and fry for a few seconds until golden. Remove from the hot oil, and drain on kitchen paper. Serve hot.

Courgette fritters

serves 6

ingredients

100g/4oz self-raising flour
2 eggs, beaten
50ml/2fl oz milk
300g/11oz courgettes, grated 2
tablespoons chopped fresh
thyme leaves
salt and freshly ground
black pepper
1 tablespoon vegetable oil

• Sift the flour into a large bowl, and make a well in the centre. Add the eggs to the well, and gradually draw in the flour from the sides using a wooden spoon.

• Slowly add the milk to the mixture, stirring constantly to form a thick batter. Add the courgettes and thyme, season with salt and pepper, and mix thoroughly.

• Heat the oil in a large heavy frying pan until hot. Cooking in batches, carefully drop in tablespoons of the batter to make the fritters. Shallow- fry for 3 minutes on each side.

• Remove the fritters with a slotted spoon, and drain on kitchen paper. Serve hot.

Soft pretzels

serves 8

ingredients

700g/1½lb plain flour; 1 tablespoon sugar; 2 teaspoons salt
2 teaspoons baking powder; 2 teaspoons active dry yeast
2 tablespoons softened butter, plus a little extra, melted; 225ml/8fl oz warm milk

- Put a large pot of water on to boil. Preheat the oven to 200°C/400°F/ Gas mark 6. Lightly grease a baking sheet.
- Put about 125g/4oz of the flour, the sugar, salt, baking powder, yeast and the 2 tablspoons softened butter in a large bowl. Mix until smooth and the yeast starts to froth.
- Sift in the remaining flour, and continue mixing until a stiff dough forms. Knead the dough until it is smooth and elastic. Form into a ball and allow to rise in a warm place until doubled in size.
- Punch down the dough and knead for a minute or so. Divide into eight equal pieces. Roll or cut each piece into a rope 45cm/18in long and 1cm/½in in diameter, and twist each rope into a pretzel shape. Allow to rest for a couple of minutes.
- Using a slotted spoon or broad spatula, slide the pretzels into the boiling water one at a time, and boil each one until they float to the top. Remove immediately, drain off and transfer to the greased baking sheet.
- Bake in the oven for 15 minutes or until golden. Brush the pretzels very lightly with melted butter as they emerge from the oven. Serve warm.

Bruschetta

serves 4

ingredients

8 slices ciabatta bread
2 garlic cloves, halved
extra virgin olive oil for drizzling 8 ripe tomatoes, sliced
8 fresh basil leaves
salt and freshly ground black pepper

- Toast the bread lightly. Rub with the garlic, cut side down, while still hot. Season with salt and lots of pepper, and drizzle enough oil on each slice to soak thoroughly.
- Divide the tomato slices evenly between the slices of bread.
- Top each bruschetta with a fresh basil leaf. Serve immediately

Cheesy stuffed peppers

serves 2-4

ingredients

2 green peppers
1 egg, hard-boiled and finely chopped
75g/3oz Cheddar cheese, grated
2 ripe tomatoes
3 tablespoons mayonnaise 2 slices of bread, toasted

• Gently simmer the peppers in a saucepan of water for 20 minutes or until tender. Drain the peppers, cool slightly, halve and deseed.

• Preheat the grill until hot. Mix the chopped eggs, cheese and tomatoes in a small bowl. Add the mayonnaise and stir well.

• Fill the pepper halves with the egg mixture, and place on the slices of toast. Cook under the hot grill until lightly browned. Serve hot.

Mini mushroom quiches

serves 6

ingredients

4 slices wholewheat bread, crusts removed; 2 teaspoons butter
225g/8oz mushrooms, wiped with damp kitchen paper and finely chopped 1 garlic clove, minced; 4 eggs; 100g/4oz Emmental cheese, grated salt and freshly ground black pepper

- Preheat the oven to 190°C/375°F/Gas mark 5.
- Roll each slice of bread with a rolling pin until flat, halve each slice and
- arrange in a greased muffin tray, pressing each slice into the cake mould. While the oven warms, bake the bread cups at a low heat until crisp and dry. Remove from the oven and set aside.
- In a small frying pan, melt the butter over a medium heat. Add the mushrooms and garlic. Sauté, stirring regularly, for 3-5 minutes until tender. Season with salt and pepper.
- Break the eggs in a bowl, piercing the yolks with a small sharp knife. Pour the eggs over the bread cups, dividing the mixture evenly. Top with the mushroom mixture, and sprinkle with the cheese.
- Bake in the oven for 15 minutes, or until the eggs are just set.

Olive cheese balls

serves 6

ingredients

225g/8oz Cheddar cheese, finely grated
300g/11oz plain flour 75g/3oz butter, melted
36 good-quality stuffed olives

- Mix together the grated cheese and flour, add the butter and mix thoroughly to form a dough. Mould 1 teaspoon of dough around each olive, and shape into a ball.
- Put the balls on a greased baking sheet. Cover and chill for 1 hour.
- Preheat the oven to 200°C/ 400°F/Gas mark 6.
- Once the balls are chilled, bake in the oven for 15-20 minutes. Serve warm.

Garlic breadsticks

serves 4

ingredients

2 baguettes
2 garlic cloves, crushed
150ml/5 fl oz olive oil

- Preheat the oven to 200°C/400°F/Gas mark 6. Cut the baguettes into three lengthways, then halve each segment, creating 12 breadsticks. Place the sticks on a baking tray.
- Mix the garlic and oil in a small bowl, then spread over the breadsticks using a pastry brush. Bake for 15-20 minutes until golden brown. Serve either hot or at room temperature.

Naan bread

serves 8

ingredients

1 teaspoon sugar; 1 teaspoon fresh yeast 150ml/5fl oz warm water; 200g/7oz plain flour 1 tablespoon ghee or butter 1 teaspoon salt; 50g/2oz unsalted butter; 1 teaspoon poppy seeds

- Put the sugar and yeast in a small bowl or jug together with the warm water, and mix thoroughly until the yeast has completely dissolved. Set aside for 10 minutes.
- Sift the flour into a large mixing bowl, making a well in the centre. Add the ghee or butter and the salt, and pour in the yeast mixture. Mix thoroughly to form a dough, adding more water if required.
- Place the dough on a floured work surface and knead until smooth. Return to the bowl, cover and set aside to rise for 1½ hours.
- Preheat the grill to very hot. Turn the dough out on to a floured surface and knead for a further 2 minutes. Break off small balls and pat them into rounds about 12.5cm/5in in diameter and 1cm/½in thick.
- Place the rounds on a greased sheet of foil, and grill for 7-10 minutes, turning twice and brushing with butter and sprinkling with poppy seeds. Serve immediately.

Garlic breadsticks

serves 4

ingredients

2 baguettes
2 garlic cloves, crushed
150ml/5 fl oz olive oil

- Preheat the oven to 200°C/400°F/Gas mark 6. Cut the baguettes into three lengthways, then halve each segment, creating 12 breadsticks. Place the sticks on a baking tray.
- Mix the garlic and oil in a small bowl, then spread over the breadsticks using a pastry brush. Bake for 15-20 minutes until golden brown. Serve either hot or at room temperature.

Crispy seaweed

serves 4

ingredients

1.1kg/21/2lb pak choi 1 teaspoon salt groundnut oil for deep-frying 1 tablespoon caster sugar

- Rinse the pak choi leaves under cold running water, then dry thoroughly with kitchen paper. Roll each pak choi leaf up and slice through thinly with a small, sharp knife, or chop using a food processor. Make sure that the leaves are finely shredded.
- Heat the groundnut oil in a large wok or frying pan until hot. Carefully add the shredded pak choi to the wok, and fry for about 30 seconds until it shrivels and becomes crispy. You may need to do this in batches.
- Remove the crispy 'seaweed' from the wok with a slotted spoon, and drain on kitchen paper. Transfer to a large bowl, toss with the salt and sugar, and serve immediately.

King prawns in sherry

serves 4

ingredients

2 tablespoons olive oil
12 raw king prawns, peeled
and deveined
2 tablespoons dry sherry
a few drops of Tabasco sauce
salt and freshly ground
black pepper
crisp lettuce leaves such as
Little
Gem, to serve

- Heat the oil in a heavy frying pan over medium-high heat, and sauté the prawns for 2-3 minutes until pink in colour.
- Pour on the sherry and Tabasco, and season with salt and pepper.
- Give the prawns a quick stir, and serve immediately on a bed of crisp lettuce leaves.

Breaded mushrooms

serves 4

ingredients

225g/8oz mushrooms, stalks removed
3 tablespoons freshly grated Parmesan cheese
4 tablespoons coarse dried white
breadcrumbs
pinch of garlic salt
pinch of ground black pepper
1 tablespoon chopped fresh flat-leaf parsley

• Preheat the oven to 240°C/ 475°F/Gas mark 9. Lightly grease a non-stick baking tray.

• Gently wipe the mushrooms with damp kitchen paper. Set aside.

• Combine the cheese with the breadcrumbs. Add the garlic salt and black pepper.

• Roll the mushrooms in the cheese mixture, and set on the greased baking tray.

• Bake in the oven for 8-10 minutes until browned. Serve hot or warm.

Melon in wine

serves 4

ingredients

2 small cantaloupe melons
175ml/6fl oz dry sparkling wine
3 tablespoons orange marmalade
½ bunch of fresh mint leaves, chopped

- Halve the melons lengthways and scoop out the seeds. Remove the flesh and cut into small cubes. Put the cubes in a bowl. Reserve the melon shells.
- In a separate small bowl, whisk together the wine, marmalade and mint. Pour the mixture over the melon flesh, and stir gently.
- Divide the mixture between the melon shells. Cover with cling film, and marinate in the refrigerator for 4-6 hours. Serve cold.

Beef carpaccio

serves 6

ingredients

350g/12oz filet mignon or similar tender cut of beef; 3 tablespoons freshly squeezed lemon juice; 1 tablespoon red wine vinegar; 75ml/3fl oz extra virgin olive oil 2 tablespoons capers, rinsed and gently squeezed dry sea salt; 200g/7oz rocket leaves, rinsed and thinly sliced, to serve ; 75g/3oz Parmesan cheese, freshly grated or shaved, to serve

- Wrap the beef in cling film; freeze for about 1 hour until firm. Cut the beef across the grain into 5mm/⅛in slices. Put the slices between two sheets of cling film, and pound with a mallet or rolling pin until paper thin. Roll the beef up in cling film once again, and chill for 1 hour.
- To make the vinaigrette, whiz the lemon juice, vinegar, oil and salt in a blender until smooth. Pour into a small bowl, and stir in the capers.
- Arrange the beef slices in a single layer on one large serving plate or six individual plates. Toss the rocket with half the dressing. Pile the rocket on top of the beef. Top with the Parmesan, and serve accompanied by the remaining dressing.

Chicken & bacon kebabs

serves 4

ingredients

2 corn on the cob
8 thick rashers back bacon
6 brown cap mushrooms, wiped with damp kitchen paper and halved
2 small chicken fillets
2 tablespoons sunflower oil
1 tablespoon freshly squeezed lemon juice
1 tablespoon maple syrup salt and freshly ground black pepper

- Cook the corn in a saucepan of boiling water until tender, then drain and cool.
- Stretch the bacon rashers using the back of a knife. Cut each rasher in half, and wrap a piece around each mushroom.
- Cut both the corn and chicken into eight equal pieces. Mix together the oil, lemon juice and syrup. Season with salt and pepper, and brush over the chicken.
- Thread the corn, bacon-wrapped mushrooms and chicken pieces alternately on skewers, and brush all over with the lemon dressing.
- Grill for 8-10 minutes, turning once and basting occasionally with any extra dressing. Serve hot.

Cauliflower fritters

serves 8

ingredients

600g/1¼lb cauliflower, cut into bite-size florets
50g/2oz chickpea flour
2 teaspoons ground cumin
1 teaspoon ground coriander 1 teaspoon ground turmeric
pinch of cayenne pepper
½ teaspoon salt
50ml/2fl oz water
1 egg plus 1 egg yolk, lightly beaten
vegetable oil for deep-frying

- Cut the cauliflower into bite-size florets. Set aside.
- Sift the flour and spices into a bowl, then stir in the ½ teaspoon salt and make a well in the centre.
- Combine 50ml/2fl oz water with the beaten egg, and gradually pour into the well, whisking to make a smooth batter. Cover and leave to rest for 30 minutes.
- Fill a deep heavy pan a third full with oil, and heat until a cube of bread browns in 15 seconds.
- Holding the florets by the stem, dip into the batter. Deep-fry in batches for 3-4 minutes until golden. Remove with a slotted spoon, and drain on kitchen paper. Serve hot.

Stuffed mushrooms

serves 4

ingredients

3 large tomatoes
8 large mushrooms with stalks, wiped with damp kitchen paper
1 small onion, grated 25g/1oz butter
1 tablespoon chopped fresh flat-leaf parsley
salt and freshly ground black pepper

- Preheat the oven to 190°C/ 375°F/Gas mark 5.
- Put the tomatoes in a bowl of just-boiled water for 30 seconds. Peel off the skins and chop the flesh.
- Remove the mushroom stalks. Chop the stalks; mix with the tomatoes, grated onion, butter and parsley. Season with salt and pepper.
- Put the mushrooms cap side down in a large greased ovenproof dish. Fill each one with the stuffing.
- Cover with foil, and bake in the oven for about 30 minutes.

Lobster rolls

serves 6

ingredients

450g/1lb lobster meat (fresh or canned)
2 celery sticks
250ml/9fl oz lemon mayonnaise
1 tablespoon chopped fresh tarragon
6 small flatbreads such as pitta
extra virgin olive oil for drizzling

- Cube the lobster meat and the celery, and put in a bowl. Stir in three-quarters of the mayonnaise and all of the tarragon.
- Warm the flatbreads under the grill. When warm but not toasted, spread with the extra mayonnaise, and scoop in the lobster mixture.
- Drizzle with extra virgin olive oil, and serve straight away.

Deep-fried fish

serves 6

ingredients

vegetable oil for deep-frying
300g/11oz plain flour
3 teaspoons salt
2 teaspoons baking powder
900g/2lb cod fillets
2 eggs
250ml/9fl oz milk
2 tablespoons olive oil

- Preheat the oil in a deep-fryer or wok to 180°C/350°F (test by frying a small cube of bread; it should brown in 30 seconds).
- In a bowl, mix together the flour, salt and baking powder. Dredge the cod fillets in the flour mixture, shaking off any excess. Reserve the remaining mixture.
- Lightly beat the eggs with the milk and olive oil. Mix in the reserved flour mixture and beat until smooth.
- Dip the cod fillets into the batter, and deep-fry until crunchy and golden brown. Drain on kitchen paper, and serve straight away.

Devilled prawns

serves 6

ingredients

2 garlic cloves, crushed
125g/4oz onions, finely chopped
1 tablespoon olive oil
4 tablespoons dry sherry
½ tablespoon fresh thyme and oregano leaves
400g/14oz cooked peeled and deveined prawns 150ml/5fl oz double cream 1 tablespoon smoked paprika salt and freshly ground
black pepper
½ tablespoon finely chopped fresh parsley, to garnish

- In a heavy saucepan or frying pan over a medium heat, sweat the garlic and onions in the oil until softened. Add the sherry, thyme and oregano, and season with salt and pepper. Cook for 2 minutes.
- Stir in the cream and let the liquid reduce a bit. Add the prawns and cook for 2 minutes, but no longer.
- Remove from the heat and serve immediately, sprinkled with the paprika and parsley.

Calamari

serves 4

ingredients

100g/4oz plain flour
1 teaspoon salt
2 eggs, beaten
175ml/6fl oz soda or sparkling mineral water
600ml/1pt vegetable oil for deep-frying
450g/1lb cleaned and prepared squid, cut into rings

• Sift the flour and salt together into a bowl. Add the eggs and half the soda or mineral water, and whisk together until smooth. Gradually whisk in the remaining soda water until the batter is smooth.

• Fill a deep heavy saucepan about one-third full with oil. Heat the oil until a cube of bread browns in 30 seconds

• Dip the squid rings into the batter, a few at a time. Carefully drop into the hot oil. Fry for 1-2 minutes until crisp and golden. Drain on kitchen paper, and serve immediately.

Prawn kebabs

serves 4-6

ingredients

1 clove garlic
1 small fresh red chilli
1 teaspoon crushed fresh root ginger
1 teaspoon granulated sugar
1 tablespoon olive oil
1 teaspoon sesame oil
1 tablespoon light soy sauce
juice of 1 lime
700g/1½lb raw prawns, peeled and deveined
175g/6oz cherry tomatoes
½ cucumber, cut into thick slices or chunks
1 bunch of fresh coriander leaves, to garnish

• Blend or process the garlic, chilli, ginger and sugar into a paste. Add the olive and sesame oils, soy sauce and lime juice. Put the prawns in a shallow glass or ceramic dish. Pour the marinade over the top. Cover and marinate in the refrigerator overnight.

• Soak bamboo skewers in cold water for at least 30 minutes to prevent them burning. Thread the skewers with the prawns, tomatoes and cucumber. Grill or barbecue for a few minutes until the prawns are pink and cooked through.

• Arrange on a platter, and garnish with coriander leaves. Serve hot.

Stilton & pear bruschetta

serves 6

ingredients

1 ciabatta loaf or ½ loaf country-style wholemeal bread, cut into at least 6 thick slices; 1 bunch of fresh watercress 75g/3oz butter, softened
2 small ripe pears such as Beurre Bosc or Comice juice of ½ lemon
200g/7oz Stilton cheese, thinly sliced freshly ground black pepper

• Preheat the oven to 200°C/ 400°F/Gas mark 6. Arrange the bread slices on a baking sheet. Toast in the oven for 10 minutes, turning halfway through the cooking time. Leave to cool.
• Strip the leaves from the watercress and chop finely, reserving a few whole leaves to garnish. Mix the chopped leaves together with the butter, and season with pepper.
• Halve the pears and remove the cores. Slice the pears thinly. Put in a bowl and add the lemon juice.
• Spread the watercress butter over the toast, then put 2 or 3 pear slices on top of each onem together with a slice of Stilton.
• Bake in the oven for about
15 minutes until the Stilton is golden brown. Cut the bruschetta into quarters, and serve on a large serving plate garnished with the reserved watercress leaves.

Grilled sardines

serves 3

ingredients

12 large fresh sardines
1 tablespoon freshly squeezed lemon juice
6 slices white bread, toasted

- Grill the sardines for a few minutes under a hot grill until tender, turning frequently.
- Trickle the lemon juice over the top of the sardines, and serve on toast while still warm.

Thai-style fish cakes

serves 4

ingredients

350g/12oz cod fillet, skinned
1 tablespoon Thai fish sauce
2 teaspoons Thai red curry paste
1 tablespoon freshly squeezed lime juice
1 garlic clove, crushed
4 fresh or dried kaffir lime leaves, crumbled
1 egg white
3 tablespoons chopped fresh coriander
125ml/4fl oz vegetable oil

- Put the cod into a blender or food processor with the fish sauce, curry paste, lime juice, garlic, lime leaves and egg white, and process until a smooth paste forms. Add the coriander and process again until mixed thoroughly.
- Divide the fish cake mixture into eight. Roll into balls, then flatten to make small round patties. (If you like, make smaller patties for canapés, but don't cook as long.)
- Heat the oil in a frying pan over a medium heat. Add the fish cakes in batches, frying for 3-4 minutes on each side until golden brown.
- Remove from the pan using a spatula, drain on kitchen paper, and serve hot.

Seared squid

serves 4

ingredients

450g/1lb shallots, thinly sliced
3 tablespoons groundnut oil
1 garlic clove, finely chopped 1
fresh red chilli, seeded
and diced
900g/2lb cleaned and prepared
squid, cut into rings salt and
freshly ground
black pepper
1 tablespoon chopped fresh
coriander leaves, to garnish

• In a heavy frying pan over a low heat, sweat the shallots in the oil for a few minutes until soft. Increase the heat and sauté, stirring, until golden and starting to crisp. Stir in the garlic and chilli. Sauté for a further 30 seconds, stirring constantly.

• Season the squid with salt and pepper. Toss into the frying pan, and sauté for 30-45 seconds until the squid curls.

• Serve immediately, garnished with the coriander leaves.

Smoked trout with cucumber & cumin

serves 4

ingredients

½ large cucumber
salt
1 tablespoon cumin seeds
250g/9oz smoked trout fillets, flaked into large pieces
150g/5oz crème fraîche

- Peel the cucumber, cut it in half lengthways and scoop out the seeds using a teaspoon. Cut the flesh into thin strips, put in a colander and sprinkle with salt. Leave for 30 minutes.
- Dry-fry the cumin seeds in a frying pan over a medium-high heat until toasted and aromatic.
- Rinse the cucumber under cold running water, drain and pat dry with kitchen paper. Put in a bowl, and sprinkle with the toasted cumin seeds. Mix in the crème fraîche.
- Serve at room temperature, with the pieces of flaked trout on top of the cucumber mixture.

Prawn cocktail

serves 4

ingredients

4 tablespoons mayonnaise
4 tablespoons single cream 2
teaspoons tomato purée
2 teaspoons lemon juice dash of
Worcestershire sauce dash of
dry sherry
salt and ground black pepper
225g/8oz peeled and deveined
cooked prawns
a few lettuce leaves, shredded
lemon slices, to garnish

• Put the mayonnaise, cream, tomato purée, lemon juice, Worcestershire sauce and sherry in a small bowl, and mix together. Season with salt and pepper.

• Add the prawns and stir well until the prawns are coated.

• To serve, put the shredded lettuce in the bottom of four glasses, and top with the prawn mixture. Garnish each prawn cocktail with lemon slices, and serve cold.

Chilli-garlic crab sticks

serves 2-4

ingredients

2 tablespoons vegetable oil
1 onion, finely chopped
2 fresh red chillies, seeded and finely chopped
2 garlic cloves, crushed
250g/9oz crab sticks
2 teaspoons light soy sauce 1 teaspoon sesame oil

• In a frying pan, a wok or a saucepan, heat the oil over a medium heat. Sauté the onion for a few minutes. Add the chillies and garlic, and continue to sauté, stirring, for a further 1 minute.

• Tip in the crab sticks and cook for 2 minutes, until they have broken up, then fold in the soy sauce and sesame oil. Serve immediately.

Prawn crackers

serves 4

ingredients

250g/9oz raw prawns, peeled and deveined
250g/9oz tapioca flour salt and freshly ground
black pepper
vegetable oil for deep-frying

- Using a blender, purée the prawns into a smooth paste. Transfer to a bowl, and mix in the tapioca flour. Season with salt and pepper. Mix well to form a stiff dough.
- Divide the dough into three equal portions. Roll each portion into a thick sausage shape (like a Swiss roll), then set the rolls on a greased plate. Using either a stand in a pan of boiling water or a steamer, steam the rolls for 40-45 minutes over a high heat.
- Leave the rolls to cool, then wrap in a clean tea towel and chill well in the refrigerator. Using a very sharp knife, slice the rolls thinly, then allow to dry out slightly.
- Heat the oil in a deep wok, and deep-fry the crackers in batches until crisp. Remove and drain on kitchen paper. Serve hot or cold.

Butterfly prawns

serves 2-4

ingredients

16 raw tiger prawns, peeled and deveined, with tails intact
juice of 2 limes
1 teaspoon cardamom seeds
2 teaspoons ground cumin
2 teaspoons ground coriander
½ teaspoon ground cinnamon
1 teaspoon ground turmeric
1 garlic clove, crushed
1 teaspoon cayenne pepper
2 tablespoons vegetable oil

• If using bamboo skewers, soak in cold water for at least 30 minutes. • Cut the prawns in half lengthways down to the tail, and flatten out to form a symmetrical shape.

• Thread a prawn onto two skewers, with the tail in the middle. Thread another 3 prawns onto the same two skewers in the same way. Repeat until you have four sets of 4 prawns on each two skewers.

• Lay the skewered prawns in a glass or ceramic dish. Sprinkle the lime juice over them. Combine the spices and oil in a small bowl, and use to coat the prawns well. Cover and chill for 2 hours.

• Cook the prawns on a foil-lined grill pan under a hot grill for 6 minutes, turning halfway through cooking. Serve immediately.

Devilled eggs with caviar

serves 4

ingredients

20 eggs, hard-boiled
6 tablespoons mayonnaise
2 tablespoons finely chopped fresh dill
100g/4oz caviar
salt and freshly ground black pepper

- Peel the hard-boiled eggs and cut in half lengthways.
- Carefully remove the yolks, and chop them finely. Put in a bowl, and add the mayonnaise and dill. Season with salt and pepper. Blend until smooth.
- Fill each half-egg with the devilled yolk mixture, and serve garnished with grains of caviar.

Bacon-wrapped prawns

serves 6

ingredients

24 large raw prawns, peeled and deveined; 24 canned whole water chestnuts, drained; 12 smoked bacon slices, halved 75g/3oz butter
250g/9oz cream cheese 125ml/4fl oz mayonnaise 125ml/4fl oz sour cream
3 tablespoons horseradish sauce 1 tablespoon freshly squeezed lemon juice

- Wrap a prawn around a water chestnut, then wrap both in a half-rasher of bacon and secure with a toothpick. Repeat the process until all the prawns, water chestnuts and bacon have been used.
- Melt 40g/½oz of the butter in a large heavy frying pan over a high heat. Add half of the prawn wraps and cook until the bacon browns. Transfer to a large dish. Repeat with the remaining butter and prawns.
- Beat the cream cheese in a medium bowl until smooth. Add the mayonnaise, sour cream, horseradish sauce and lemon juice, and blend thoroughly. Spoon the sauce over the prawn wraps.
- Grill under a medium heat until golden brown. Serve immediately.

Smoked salmon rolls

serves 6

ingredients

200g/7oz ricotta cheese 50g/2oz crème fraîche; 2 teaspoon wasabi paste
1 tablespoon freshly squeezed lime juice
12 slices brown bread, crusts removed
300g/11oz smoked salmon 100g/4oz baby rocket leaves, stalks removed

- Mix together the ricotta, crème fraîche, wasabi and lime juice. Use a rolling pin to flatten the bread slices slightly.
- Spread the ricotta mixture over the bread, then top with the smoked salmon and rocket leaves, leaving a border around the edges.
- Roll each piece of bread up lengthways like a Swiss roll. Wrap the rolls tightly in cling film, and chill in the refrigerator for 30 minutes.
- Unwrap the rolls and cut into 2.5cm/1in slices to serve.

Asparagus & chorizo salad

serves 4

ingredients

250g/9oz asparagus; 2 chorizo sausages, sliced into bite-size pieces
3 tablespoons olive oil; ½ tablespoon sherry vinegar
1 tablespoon wholegrain mustard salt and freshly ground black pepper
2 slices white bread, crusts removed, cut into
1cm/½in cubes handful of rocket leaves

- Cook the asparagus in salted boiling water for about 10 minutes until tender. Drain, then refresh in cold water. Leave to cool.
- Grill the chorizo for 5 minutes under a hot grill. Leave to cool on kitchen paper.
- Combine 2 tablespoons of the olive oil with the sherry vinegar, mustard, salt and pepper.
- Heat the remaining olive oil in a pan and add the bread cubes. Fry until crisp and golden.
- Serve the asparagus on top of the rocket salad. Scatter with the chorizo and croûtons, and pour the dressing over the top.

Courgettes stuffed with mince

serves 4

ingredients

8 medium courgettes
450g/1lb minced beef 1 egg
2 garlic cloves, crushed
½ teaspoon dried mixed herbs
4 tablespoons fresh breadcrumbs
2 tablespoons water

- Pre-heat the oven to 180°C/ 350°F/Gas mark 4.
- Cut each of the courgettes in half lengthways. Using a sharp knife or teaspoon, scoop out the courgette flesh to make shells, taking care not to pierce the skin.
- Mix together all the remaining ingredients in a bowl. Spoon the mixture into the courgette halves and rejoin each half to another to form whole courgettes again.
- Put the filled courgettes in a lightly oiled baking dish, and roast in the oven for 30 minutes. Serve hot.

Beef satay

serves 4

ingredients

900g/2lb rump steak, cut into cubes
75ml/3fl oz black bean sauce 2 tablespoons vegetable oil

• Soak 4 bamboo skewers for at least 30 minutes.
• Thread the steak cubes onto the skewers, and brush with the black bean sauce.
• Heat the oil in a ridged grill pan over a medium-high heat. Grill the satay for 2-3 minutes on each side, brushing with any leftover black bean sauce. Serve hot.

Moroccan lamb koftas

serves 4

ingredients

450g/1lb minced lamb 2 eggs, lightly beaten 200g/7oz stale coarse fresh breadcrumbs 2 onions, grated 2 tablespoons chopped fresh flat-leaf parsley ½ teaspoon ground cinnamon 1 teaspoon ground cumin ½ teaspoon chilli powder 2 teaspoons ground turmeric 1 teaspoon ground allspice

For the yogurt sauce 50ml/2fl oz Greek-style yogurt 2 teaspoons freshly squeezed lemon juice 2 tablespoons tahini paste 1 garlic clove, crushed

- In a blender or food processor, purée all the ingredients until smooth and paste-like. Divide the lamb mixture into two portions, and mould each half around a separate metal skewer to form two long sausage shapes.
- Just before serving, grill or barbecue both of the koftas until browned and cooked through, turning from time to time while cooking.
- Combine all the ingredients for the yogurt sauce in a small bowl. Add 2 tablespoons water, mix well and serve with the hot or warm koftas.

Devils on horseback

serves 3

ingredients

3 bacon rashers, cut into thin strips
12 pitted prunes
1½ teaspoons Tabasco sauce

• Soak 12 toothpicks in cold water for 30 minutes to prevent them burning. Wrap a piece of bacon around each prune, and secure with a toothpick.
• Preheat the grill until hot. Grill the prunes, turning occasionally, until the bacon is crisp.
• Serve hot, sprinkled with the Tabasco sauce.

Mixed bhajias

serves 4

ingredients

175g/6oz gram flour 1 teaspoon bicarbonate of soda 2 teaspoons ground coriander 1 teaspoon garam masala 1½ teaspoons ground turmeric 1½ teaspoons chilli powder 2 tablespoons chopped fresh coriander 1 small onion, halved and sliced 1 small leek, sliced 100g/4oz cauliflower, blanched vegetable oil for deep-frying For the sauce
150ml/5fl oz Greek-style yogurt 2 tablespoons chopped fresh mint ½ teaspoon ground turmeric 1 garlic clove, crushed

- Sift the flour and bicarbonate of soda into a mixing bowl, add the spices and fresh coriander, and mix thoroughly. Divide the mixture between three separate small bowls. Stir the onion into one bowl, the leek into another and the cauliflower into the third. Add 4 tablespoons cold water to each bowl, and mix each one to form a smooth paste.
- Heat enough oil for deep-frying in a wok or heavy pan. Using two tablespoons, form the mixture into rounds. Cooking in batches, fry the bhajias in the oil until golden brown. Remove with a slotted spoon and drain on kitchen paper.
- Mix all the sauce ingredients together, and pour into a small serving bowl. Serve with the warm bhajias.

Minced beef with eggs

serves 6

ingredients

1 onion, finely chopped
40g/1½oz butter
450g/1lb minced beef
1 green pepper, sliced
2 tomatoes, peeled, seeded and diced
2 tablespoons chopped fresh flat-leaf parsley 6 eggs
salt and freshly ground black pepper

• Sweat the onion in the butter for about 10 minutes until starting to caramelize. Add the minced beef, and continue to cook, stirring, until the meat browns.

• Stir in the green pepper and diced tomato. Cook for 2 minutes. Mix in the parsley, and season with salt and pepper. Cover the pan, and simmer for about 8 minutes.

• Make six holes in the meat in the pan, and break an egg into each space. Cover and cook for about 5 minutes until the egg whites are cooked through. Serve hot.

Chicken saltimbocca

serves 6

ingredients

3 skinless chicken breast
fillets, halved lengthways
6 thin slices boiled ham
6 slices Emmenthal cheese
1 tomato, thinly sliced
1 teaspoon crushed dried sage
75g/3oz fine dried
breadcrumbs 2 tablespoons
freshly grated
Parmesan cheese
2 tablespoons chopped fresh
flat-leaf parsley 50g/2oz
butter, melted

- Preheat the oven to 180°C/ 350°F/Gas mark 4.
- Put the chicken fillets, bottom side up, between two pieces of cling film. Working out from the centre, pound each piece lightly with a meat mallet. Remove the cling film. Put a ham slice, a cheese slice and a few tomato slices on each piece.
- Sprinkle each fillet lightly with the sage, and roll up Swiss-roll style. Press to seal well.
- Combine the breadcrumbs, Parmesan and parsley. Dip the chicken in the butter, then roll in the breadcrumbs. Bake in a lightly oiled dish for 40-45 minutes.

Chicken liver pâté

serves 4

ingredients

450g/1lb chicken livers
50g/2oz butter
1 teaspoon brandy
2 eggs, hard-boiled
1 onion, roughly chopped

• Clean the livers thoroughly. Fry in a large frying pan over a medium-high heat with the butter and brandy.

• In a blender or food processor, purée the livers, eggs, onion and any cooking juices in the pan. Transfer the mixture to a serving dish. Cover with foil, then put a weight such as a plate on top. Chill overnight.

• Serve at room temperature

Crab pâté

serves 10

ingredients

275g/10oz canned cream of mushroom soup
1 tablespoon powdered gelatine
100g/4oz mayonnaise 225g/8oz cream cheese, softened
350g/12oz cooked crabmeat
1 small onion, finely chopped
100g/4oz celery, finely chopped
½ teaspoon dried dill

- Heat the soup in a medium heavy saucepan over a low heat. Remove from the heat.
- In a small bowl, dissolve the gelatine in 3 tablespoons cold water. Add to the soup, stirring well until completely combined. Add the remaining ingredients and mix thoroughly.
- Spoon into an oiled 1.2-litre/2pt mould, and chill until firm.

Smoked mackerel pâté

serves 4

ingredients

1 smoked mackerel fillet,
skinned 50g/2oz cottage cheese
60ml/21?2 fl oz sour cream
½ teaspoon dried fennel
½ teaspoon dried dill juice of 1
lemon
salt and freshly ground
black pepper freshly grated
nutmeg

- Purée the mackerel in a food processor or blender.
- Add the cottage cheese, sour cream, lemon juice, fennel and dill. Continue blending until smooth, stirring occasionally.
- Spoon the mixture into a bowl. Season with salt, pepper and nutmeg to taste.
- Divide the mixture among four individual pots or dishes, cover and chill for 24 hours.

Pork & liver pâté

serves 8

ingredients

350g/12oz streaky bacon rashers 225g/8oz pork shoulder, roughly chopped
225g/8oz pork sausagemeat 225g/8oz pig's liver, chopped 1 small onion 2 garlic cloves
1 tablespoon chopped fresh oregano 1 tablespoon chopped fresh thyme 3 tablespoons marsala
salt and ground black pepper

- Preheat the oven to 170°C/325°F/Gas mark 3.
- Grease a 450g/1lb loaf tin. Line with the bacon rashers, reserving a few for the top.
- Put the pork shoulder in a food processor and chop until fine. Add the remaining ingredients, and blend for 30 seconds until smooth.
- Add the mixture to the loaf tin, smooth the top and cover with the reserved bacon rashers. Cover with foil.
- Put the loaf tin in a larger baking tray half-filled with boiling water. Carefully transfer to the oven, and bake for 1½ hours or until firm. Remove from the oven and take off the foil. Cover the pâté with greaseproof paper, and set a heavy weight on top such as a plate. Chill overnight in the refrigerator. Serve in slices at room temperature.

Pâté en croûte

serves 8

ingredients

450g/1lb streaky bacon rashers 250g/9oz chicken livers, cleaned and finely minced 1 onion, finely chopped 1 garlic clove, crushed 2 tablespoons fresh white breadcrumbs 3 tablespoons sherry 1 teaspoon freshly grated nutmeg 200g/7oz ready-made puff pastry 1 egg, beaten freshly ground black pepper

- Preheat the oven to 180°C/350°F/Gas mark 4.
- Set aside 6 rashers of the bacon to line the pâté tin. Remove and discard the rinds from the remaining bacon rashers, and chop finely.
- Mix the rindless rashers with the chicken liver in a large bowl. Stir in the onion, garlic, breadcrumbs, sherry, nutmeg and black pepper to taste.
- Stretch the remaining rashers of bacon across the bottom and sides of a 1.1kg/2lb loaf tin, reserving 2 for the top. Spoon in the pâté mixture, and place 2 rashers on top.
- Cover with foil, and stand the pâté tin in a shallow roasting tin half-filled with hot water. Bake in the oven for 30 minutes until the pâté has shrunk away from the sides of the tin.
- Remove the pâté tin from the hot water, and pour off the excess fat. Leave to stand for 15 minutes.
- Increase the oven temperature to 200°C/400°F/Gas mark 6.
- Roll out the pastry thinly. Turn the pâté out of its tin, and brush with some of the beaten egg. Cover with the pastry, using the beaten egg to seal the edges and to brush the outside of the pastry case.
- Carefully place on an oiled baking sheet, and cook in the oven for a further 30 minutes until the pastry is golden brown. Remove from the oven, and allow to cool before serving.

Dolmades

serves 4

ingredients

1 tablespoon olive oil 100g/4oz minced beef 2 tablespoons pine nuts 1 onion, chopped 1 tablespoon chopped fresh coriander leaves 1 teaspoon ground cumin 1 tablespoon tomato purée 8 preserved vine leaves salt and freshly ground black pepper
For the tomato sauce: 150ml/5fl oz passata 150ml/5fl oz beef stock 2 teaspoons caster sugar

- To make the filling, heat the oil in a pan over a medium heat. Add the minced beef, pine nuts and onion. Cook, stirring, for 5 minutes until the meat has browned and sealed.
- Stir in the fresh coriander, cumin and tomato purée. Cook for a further 3 minutes, then season well with salt and pepper. Remove from the heat and set aside.
- Rinse the vine leaves, and lay them shiny side down on a work surface. Put some of the filling in the centre of each leaf, and fold the stalk end over the filling. Roll up each parcel towards the tip of the leaf, and put in a lightly greased flameproof casserole dish, seam side down.
- To make the tomato sauce, mix together the passata, stock and sugar, and pour over the vine leaves, making sure that each one is covered. Cover the casserole, and cook over a medium heat for a few minutes. Reduce the heat, and cook gently for a further 30 minutes. Serve hot.

Cheesy potato skins

serves 4

ingredients

3 baking potatoes, scored into quarters 1 teaspoon vegetable oil 50g/2oz lean smoked back bacon, roughly chopped 175g/6oz brown cap mushrooms, roughly chopped 100g/4oz cream cheese, softened 2 tablespoons milk 1½ teaspoons wholegrain mustard 50g/2oz Cheddar cheese, grated

- Preheat the oven to 200°C/400°F/Gas mark 6. Put the potatoes in a baking dish, and bake in the oven for 1 hour or until cooked.
- Meanwhile, heat the oil in a frying pan over a medium heat, and sauté the bacon until cooked. Add the mushrooms and continue to sauté until any excess moisture has evaporated. Remove from the heat. Blend the cream cheese, milk, mustard and half of the Cheddar cheese in a bowl.
- When the potatoes are cooked, quarter them and scrape out the inside, leaving a thin layer of potato on the skin. Put the potato flesh to one side. Put the skins on a baking tray, and return to the oven for 5 minutes.
- Mash the potato flesh, and stir into the cheese mixture with the cooked bacon and mushrooms. Pile the mixture into the potato skins, and sprinkle the remaining cheese over the top.
- Return the potato skins to the oven for 10 minutes or until golden brown. Serve hot.

Cheesy garlic bread

serves 4-6

ingredients

100g/4oz butter, melted
4 garlic cloves, crushed
¼ teaspoon dried oregano
1 baguette, halved lengthways 3 tablespoons freshly grated Parmesan cheese

• In a small bowl, combine the butter, garlic and oregano. Spread the mixture over the cut sides of the baguette.

• Sprinkle the bread with Parmesan, and place on an ungreased baking sheet. Grill under a high heat for 3 minutes or until golden brown. Slice and serve hot.

Salmon-filled mushroom caps

serves 6

ingredients

200g/7oz canned salmon 25g/1oz fine dried breadcrumbs 2 tablespoons chopped onion 2 tablespoons chopped fresh flat-leaf parsley 18 large fresh mushrooms, caps about 4cm/11? 2in diameter 2 tablespoons red pepper, diced pinch of salt and freshly ground black pepper

- Preheat the oven to 180°C/350°F/Gas mark 4.
- In a small mixing bowl, combine the salmon, breadcrumbs, onion and parsley. Season with a pinch of salt and pepper.
- Remove the stalks from the mushrooms, and wipe the mushroom caps with damp kitchen paper. Put in a baking tray, crown side down. Mould the salmon mixture into the caps. Put a little red pepper on top of each cap.
- Bake for 15-20 minutes until tender. Serve hot.

Salmon yakitori

serves 4

ingredients

350g/12oz salmon fillet, skinned and cut into 5cm/2in chunks 8 baby leeks, trimmed and cut into 5cm/2in lengths

For the sauce

75ml/3fl oz light soy sauce 75ml/3fl oz fish stock 25g/1oz caster sugar 75ml/3fl oz dry white wine 50ml/2fl oz sweet sherry 1 garlic clove, crushed

- Soak 8 bamboo skewers in cold water for at least 30 minutes. Thread the salmon and leeks alternately onto the soaked skewers. Leave in the refrigerator until needed.
- To make the sauce, put all the ingredients in a small saucepan, and heat gently over a low heat, stirring, until the sugar dissolves. Bring to the boil, then reduce the heat and simmer for 2 minutes. Strain the sauce and leave to cool. Pour about one-third of the sauce into a small dish.
- Heat a barbecue or grill until medium-hot. Brush plenty of the remaining sauce over the kebabs, and cook for 10 minutes, basting frequently with the sauce. Serve hot with the reserved sauce for dipping.

Melon with Parma ham

serves 6

ingredients

1 honeydew melon, cut into
6 wedges and seeds removed
6 slices wafer-thin Parma ham 6 cherry tomatoes

- • Remove the peel from the melon, and cut each wedge into two thin wedges. Halve the ham slices widthways.
- • Wrap a piece of ham round the centre of each piece of melon, and arrange the wedges on serving plates. Garnish each serving with a cherry tomato. Serve.

Prawn & sesame seed toast

serves 4

ingredients

225g/8oz peeled and deveined cooked prawns 1 spring onion ¼ teaspoon salt 1 teaspoon light soy sauce 1 tablespoon cornflour 1 egg white, beaten 3 thin slices white bread, crusts removed 4 tablespoons sesame seeds 600ml/1pt vegetable oil for deep-frying

• Put the prawns and spring onion in a blender or food processor, and whiz until finely chopped. Transfer to a bowl, and stir in the salt, soy sauce, cornflour and egg white.

• Spread the mixture on to one side of each slice of bread. Spread the sesame seeds on top of the mixture, pressing down well. Cut each slice into four equal triangles.

• Heat the vegetable oil in a wok over a medium-high heat.

• Carefully lower the triangles into the oil, coated side down, and fry for 2-3 minutes until golden brown. Remove with a slotted spoon, and drain on kitchen paper. Serve immediately.

Cheese & spinach puffs

serves 6

ingredients

150g/5oz cooked spinach, chopped 175g/6oz cottage cheese 1 teaspoon freshly grated nutmeg 2 egg whites 25g/1oz Parmesan cheese, freshly grated salt and freshly ground black pepper

- Preheat the oven to 220°C/425°F/Gas mark 7, and lightly oil six individual ramekins.
- In a small bowl, mix together the spinach and cottage cheese. Sprinkle in the nutmeg, and season with salt and pepper. Stir through.
- Whisk the egg whites in a separate bowl until stiff enough to hold soft peaks. Fold the egg whites evenly into the spinach mixture using a large metal spoon, then spoon the mixture into the prepared ramekins. Smooth the tops using the back of the spoon.
- Sprinkle with the Parmesan, and place the ramekins on a baking tray. Bake for 15-20 minutes until well risen. Serve immediately.

Baked mozzarella & tomatoes

serves 5

ingredients

6 beefsteak tomatoes, sliced
100g/4oz mozzarella cheese, grated
6 black olives, stoned and sliced
12 fresh basil leaves
1 tablespoon extra virgin olive oil
1 tablespoon freshly squeezed lemon juice
2 slices white bread, diced

- Preheat the oven to 200°C/ 400°F/Gas mark 6.
- Lay the tomato slices, overlapping them slightly, in six individual shallow ovenproof dishes.
- Sprinkle the cheese, olives and basil leaves over the top. Add a few drops of olive oil to each, then a small splash of lemon juice.
- Put the bread on a baking tray, and place both the bread and the individual dishes in the oven. Bake for 8-10 minutes. Sprinkle the croûtons over the cheese, and serve hot.

Baked fennel

serves 4

ingredients

2 fennel bulbs
2 celery sticks, cut into 7.5cm/3in lengths
6 sun-dried tomatoes, halved
200g/7oz passata
2 teaspoons dried oregano
50g/2oz Parmesan cheese, freshly grated

- Preheat the oven to 190°C/ 375°F/Gas mark 5.
- Using a sharp knife, trim the fennel, discarding any tough outer leaves, and cut the bulb into quarters.
- Bring a large saucepan of water to the boil, add the fennel and celery, and simmer for 8-10 minutes until just tender. Remove with a slotted spoon, and leave to drain.
- Put the fennel, celery and sun-dried tomatoes in a large ovenproof dish. Mix the passata and oregano together, and pour the mixture over the fennel in the dish.
- Sprinkle the Parmesan over the top, and bake in the oven for 20 minutes. Serve hot.

Greek-style tomato platter

serves 6

ingredients

8 tomatoes, sliced
100g/4oz feta cheese, crumbled
8 black olives, stoned and sliced
1 tablespoon chopped fresh oregano
1 tablespoon white wine vinegar 1 tablespoon olive oil

- Arrange the tomato slices on six small serving plates or one large serving platter. Scatter the cheese, olives and oregano on top.
- Whisk together the vinegar and oil and drizzle over the top of the salad. Serve immediately.

Fruit cocktail

serves 6

ingredients

½ honeydew melon 225g/8oz
canned pineapple
chunks in juice 225g/8oz
seedless white
grapes, halved
125ml/4fl oz white grape juice

• Remove the seeds from the melon half, and use a melon baller to scoop out even-sized balls.

• Combine all the fruits in a glass bowl, and pour the pineapple and grape juices over the top.

• Cover and chill until required.

Griddled smoked salmon

serves 4

ingredients

350g/12oz sliced smoked salmon
1 teaspoon Dijon mustard
1 garlic clove, crushed
2 teaspoons chopped fresh dill 2 teaspoons sherry vinegar
4 tablespoons olive oil
salt and freshly ground black pepper
100g/4oz mixed salad leaves

- Fold the slices of smoked salmon, making two folds, accordion-style, so that they form little parcels.
- To make the vinaigrette, whisk the mustard, garlic, dill, vinegar and oil together in a small bowl. Season with salt and pepper.
- Heat a ridged grill pan over a medium heat until smoking. Add the salmon parcels, and cook on one side only for 2-3 minutes until heated through.
- Meanwhile, dress the salad leaves with some of the vinaigrette, and divide between four serving plates.
- Top the salad with the smoked salmon, cooked side up. Drizzle with the remaining vinaigrette, and serve immediately.

Chicken tikka

serves 6

ingredients

450g/1lb skinless chicken breast or thigh fillet, cubed
1 teaspoon grated fresh root ginger
1 garlic clove, crushed
1 teaspoon chilli powder
¼ teaspoon ground turmeric
1 teaspoon salt
150ml/5fl oz low-fat Greek-style yogurt
50ml/2fl oz freshly squeezed lemon juice
1 tablespoon chopped fresh coriander leaves
1 tablespoon sunflower oil

- In a medium bowl, mix together all the ingredients except the sunflower oil. Leave to marinate in the refrigerator for at least 2 hours.
- Preheat the grill to medium. Lay the marinated chicken on a grill tray in a flameproof dish lined with foil, and baste with the oil.
- Once the grill is hot enough, grill the chicken for 15-20 minutes until cooked, turning and basting three times during the cooking process. Serve hot.

Artichoke & prawn cocktail

serves 6

ingredients

900g/2lb canned artichoke hearts, drained and quartered
225g/8oz peeled and deveined cooked prawns
3 tablespoons olive oil
2 tablespoons freshly squeezed lemon juice
150ml/5fl oz sour cream salt and freshly ground black pepper

- Put the artichokes in a bowl, and add the prawns. Drizzle the oil and lemon juice over the top, and season with a little salt and lots of pepper. Toss gently and chill until ready to serve.
- Just before serving, spoon the mixture into six wine goblets. Top each one with a spoonful of sour cream, and serve.

Sweetcorn pancakes

serves 4

ingredients

100g/4oz self-raising flour
1 egg white
150ml/5fl oz skimmed milk
200g/7oz canned sweetcorn kernels, drained vegetable oil for brushing salt and freshly ground black pepper

- Put the flour, egg white and milk in a blender or food processor with half the sweetcorn, and purée until a smooth paste forms.
- Season well with salt and pepper, and add the remaining sweetcorn.
- Heat a heavy frying pan over a medium heat, and brush with oil. Drop in tablespoons of the batter, and cook until set and the bottom is golden. Turn over and cook on the other side. Serve hot.

Avocado cream

serves 4

ingredients

1 tablespoon powdered gelatine
150ml/5fl oz vegetable stock
1 large avocado
2 teaspoons freshly squeezed lemon juice
4 tablespoons low-calorie mayonnaise
1 teaspoon Worcestershire sauce 1 teaspoon Tabasco sauce
2 tablespoons snipped fresh chives

- In a small bowl, mix the gelatine with 50ml/2fl oz cold water, and leave to soften for a few minutes. Stand the bowl in a pan of gently simmering water, and stir until the gelatine completely dissolves. Stir in the stock and leave to cool.
- Halve the avocado, remove the stone and scoop the flesh into a bowl. Mash well with the lemon juice. Beat in the mayonnaise, and flavour with the Worcestershire and Tabasco sauces. Stir in the chives. Stir the cooled stock into the avocado mixture.
- Divide between four small dishes and chill until set. Serve cold.

Sweet & sour baby onions

serves 4

ingredients

350g/12oz baby onions
2 tablespoons olive oil
2 fresh bay leaves, torn into strips thinly pared zest of 1 lemon
1 tablespoon Demerara sugar
1 tablespoon clear honey
4 tablespoons red wine vinegar

• Soak the onions in a bowl of boiling water for 15 minutes. Using a sharp knife, peel and halve the onions.
• Heat the oil in a large frying pan over medium-high heat. Add the onions and bay leaves to the pan, and cook for 5-6 minutes until golden brown all over.
• Slice the lemon zest into thin matchsticks. Add to the frying pan with the sugar and honey. Cook for 2-3 minutes, stirring occasionally, until the onions are lightly caramelized.
• Add the vinegar to the frying pan. Continue to cook for 5 minutes or so, stirring, until the onions are tender. Transfer to a dish, and serve immediately.

Stuffed celery

serves 4

ingredients

225g/8oz low-fat cottage cheese
2 teaspoons freshly squeezed lemon juice
½ teaspoon light soy sauce
1 teaspoon prepared mustard
50g/2oz seeded red pepper, chopped
50g/2oz chives, chopped
1 garlic clove, crushed
6 celery sticks, leaves removed

- Put all the ingredients except the celery into a blender or food processor, and purée until smooth.
- Stuff the celery sticks with the cheese mixture. Refrigerate for at least 30 minutes before serving.

Parma ham & pepper pizzas

serves 4

ingredients

1 red pepper
1 yellow pepper
½ loaf ciabatta bread
4 slices Parma ham, cut into thick strips
50g/2oz reduced-fat mozzarella
cheese, thinly sliced

• Grill the peppers for 5 minutes or so until their skins are charred. When cool enough to handle, peel off and discard the skin and seeds.
• Cut the bread into 4 thick slices, and toast until golden.
• Cut the peppers into thick strips, and arrange on the bread with the Parma ham.
• Preheat the grill until medium-hot. • Arrange the mozzarella on top of the pizzas. Grill for 2-3 minutes
until the cheese is melted and bubbling. Serve hot.

Crab & cucumber savouries

serves 6

ingredients

1 large cucumber, seeded if necessary and diced
50g/2oz low-fat spread
225g/8oz button mushrooms, sliced
2 teaspoons plain flour
150ml/5fl oz fish stock, made with ½ stock cube
1 tablespoon dry sherry
75ml/3fl oz low-fat single cream 175g/6oz canned cooked white crabmeat
salt and freshly ground black pepper

- Boil the cucumber in lightly salted water for 3 minutes, then drain well. In the same pan, melt the low- fat spread. Cook the mushrooms, stirring, for 2 minutes.
- Add the cucumber, cover and cook over a gentle heat for 2 minutes.
- Stir in the flour, remove from the heat and, while still stiriring, add the stock, sherry and cream.
- Return to the heat, bring to the boil and cook for 2 minutes, stirring.
- Add the crabmeat, and season with salt and pepper.
- Heat through, then spoon into six serving dishes. Serve hot.

Devilled eggs

serves 4

ingredients

100g/4oz low-fat cottage cheese 50g/2oz low-fat mayonnaise 50g/2oz onion, finely diced 50g/2oz celery, finely diced)
¼ teaspoon celery seed
¼ teaspoon salt
1 teaspoon Dijon mustard
8 eggs, hard-boiled, halved with
yolks removed
2 tablespoons chopped fresh flat-leaf parsley

• In a medium bowl, beat the cottage cheese and mayonnaise until fluffy. Add all the remaining ingredients, except for the egg white halves and the parsley, and beat well once again.

• Stuff the eggs with the devilled mixture, and chill until needed.

• Just before serving, scatter the eggs with the parsley.

Note If you like, you can use the egg yolks in the devilled mixture. Simply chop finely and add with the other ingredients – although this will increase the calories.

Pineapple boats

serves 6

ingredients

1 pineapple
225g/8oz low-fat cottage cheese
1 red pepper, seeded and chopped
1 fresh green chilli, seeded and chopped
salt and freshly ground black pepper

- Cut the pineapple into six wedges, then cut most of the flesh from the skin and roughly chop, discarding any tough central core. Reserve the wedges of skin.
- Put the pineapple flesh in a bowl with the cottage cheese, red pepper and chilli. Mix well and season with salt and black pepper.
- Lay the wedges of pineapple skin flesh-side down on a work surface. Spoon the cheese mixture onto the skins, and chill for at least 1 hour before serving.

Tomato & cheese tarts

serves 4

ingredients

2 sheets filo pastry
1 egg white
100g/4oz low-fat soft cheese
handful of fresh basil leaves 3
small tomatoes, sliced
salt and freshly ground
black pepper

• Preheat the oven to 200°C/400°F/ Gas mark 6.
• Brush the sheets of filo pastry lightly with the egg white, and cut into 16 squares, each measuring about 10cm/4in.
• Layer the squares in twos, in eight patty tins. Spoon the cheese into the pastry cases.
• Season with salt and pepper, and top with the basil leaves.
• Arrange the tomatoes on the tarts, and season again with salt and pepper. Bake for 10-12 minutes until golden. Serve warm.

Succotash

serves 4-6

ingredients

4 tablespoons vegetable oil
500g/1lb 2oz lean smoked bacon rashers, cut into squares
1 large onion, finely sliced
3 garlic cloves, finely chopped 1 red pepper, seeded and chopped
1 green pepper, seeded and chopped
900g/2lb canned red kidney beans, drained
1.4kg/3lb sweetcorn kernels 3 tomatoes, diced
150g/5oz Parmesan cheese, freshly grated

• Heat the oil in a heavy saucepan over a high heat, and sauté the bacon until browned.
• Reduce the heat and add the onion, garlic, peppers, kidney beans and sweetcorn. Pour in 350ml/12fl oz water. Stir well.
• Simmer the succotash over a low heat for 15 minutes, then add the tomatoes. Continue to simmer for a further 20 minutes or until the sauce has reduced.
• Sprinkle the succotash with the cheese, and serve hot.

Thank you!

For purchasing this book. Your order made our day! We hope we make yours

If you have any questions about this book, contact us anytime. We'd love to hear from you. Are you happy with your book?

Yes ☺

Great! Than please share your review online

No ☹

Please contact us at sootiecharitys@yahoo.com

CPSIA information can be obtained
at www.ICGtesting.com
Printed in the USA
LVHW060036171121
703501LV00009B/182

9 781803 892641